D1180711

For my parents

First published 1988 by Walker Books Ltd
87 Vauxhall Walk, London SE11 5HJ

Special New Edition published 1997
This edition published 1998

2 4 6 8 10 9 7 5 4 3 1

© 1988, 1994, 1997 Martin Handford

The right of Martin Handford to be identified as author/illustrator
of this work has been asserted by him in accordance with the
Copyright, Designs and Patents Act 1988.

Printed in Italy

British Library Cataloguing in Publication Data
A catalogue record for this book is
available from the British Library.

ISBN 0-7445-6167-1

WHERE'S WALLY NOW?

MARTIN HANDFORD

WALKER BOOKS
AND SUBSIDIARIES
LONDON · BOSTON · SYDNEY

HI THERE, BOOK WORMS!

SOME BITS OF HISTORY ARE AMAZING!
I SIT HERE READING ALL THESE BOOKS
ABOUT THE WORLD LONG AGO, AND IT'S
LIKE RIDING A TIME MACHINE. WHY NOT
TRY IT FOR YOURSELVES? JUST SEARCH
EACH PICTURE AND FIND ME, WOOF
(REMEMBER, ALL YOU CAN SEE IS HIS TAIL),
WENDA, WIZARD WHITEBEARD AND ODLAW.
THEN LOOK FOR MY KEY, WOOF'S BONE (IN
THIS SCENE IT'S THE BONE THAT'S
NEAREST TO HIS TAIL), WENDA'S CAMERA,
WIZARD WHITEBEARD'S SCROLL AND
ODLAW'S BINOCULARS.

THERE ARE ALSO 25 WALLY-WATCHERS,
EACH OF WHOM APPEARS ONLY ONCE
SOMEWHERE ON MY TRAVELS. AND ONE
MORE THING! CAN YOU FIND ANOTHER
CHARACTER, NOT SHOWN BELOW, WHO
APPEARS ONCE IN EVERY PICTURE?

Wally

THE RIDDLE OF THE PYRAMIDS

The Ancient Egyptians were very clever people who loved goats, cats and sphinx, and invented pyramids. With great difficulty they built several huge pyramids in the desert. But now no one can remember why. Were they adventure playgrounds for Egyptian mummies and babies, or were they houses without any of the useful bits?

Is it possible (or even likely) that Pharaohs were buried under them? These questions are as hard to answer as a camel's hump.

FUN AND GAMES IN ANCIENT ROME

The Romans spent most of their time fighting, conquering, learning Latin and making roads. When they took their holidays, they always had games at the Coliseum (an old sort of playground). Their favourite games were fighting, more fighting, chariot racing, fighting and feeding Christians to lions. When the crowd gave a gladiator the thumbs down, it meant kill your opponent. Thumbs up meant let him go, to fight to the death another day.

1,003 YEARS AGO

ON TOUR WITH THE VIKINGS

At home the Vikings were quiet people who liked knitting and cheese tasting and boring things like that. But on tour they went wild. They put on their best horned hats and sailed across the sea, singing and shouting like mad. If you heard them coming, it was best to run away, because once they had arrived and unpacked their axes, there was no holding them back.

800 YEARS AGO

THE END
OF THE
CRUSADES

After 200 years of fierce argument with the Saladins and Paladins, who would not tell them the way to Jerusalem, the Crusaders finally ran out of clean T-shirts, so they came home. For years afterwards they dined out on stories of the lovely castles they had battered and besieged and the fascinating people they had thrown rocks at, so the Crusades were not a complete waste of time after all.

ONCE UPON A SATURDAY MORNING

The Middle Ages were a very merry time to be alive, especially on Saturdays, as long as you didn't get caught. Short skirts and stripy tights were in fashion for men; everybody knew lots of jokes; there was widespread juggling and jousting and archery and jesting and fun. But if you got into trouble, the Middle Ages could be miserable. For the man in the stocks or the pillory or about to lose his head, Saturday morning was no laughing matter.

THE LAST DAYS OF THE AZTECS

The Aztecs lived in sunny Mexico and were rich and strong and liked swinging from poles pretending to be eagles. They also liked making human sacrifices to their gods, so it was best to agree with everything they said. The Spanish were also rich and strong, and some of them, called conquistadors, came to Mexico in 1519 to have an adventure. They thought the Aztecs were a complete nuisance, only good for arguing with and fighting.

TROUBLE IN OLD JAPAN

400 YEARS AGO

Is red better than blue? What do you mean your poem about cherry blossom is better than mine? Shall we have another cup of tea? Over difficult questions such as these, the Japanese fought fiercely for hundreds of years. The fiercest fighters of all were the samurai, who wore flags on their backs so that their mummies could find them. The fighters without flags were called ashigaru. They couldn't take a joke any better than the samurai, especially about their hair.

BEING A PIRATE

(Shiver-me-timbers!)

It was really a lot of fun being a pirate, especially if you were very hairy and didn't have much in the way of brains. It also helped if you only had one leg, or one eye, or two noses, and had a pirate's hat with your name-tag sewn inside and a treasure-map and a rusty cutlass. Once there were lots of pirates, but they died out in the end because too many of them were men (which is not a good idea).

HAVING A BALL
IN
GAYE PAREE

The history of France has some very bad bits, like getting your head chopped off by Madame Guillotine in the French Revolution; and some very good bits, like the invention of smelly cheese. In 1870 Napoleon (the third one) threw a marvellous ball in Paris to celebrate 1870 being a good bit. All the beautiful people came and danced the night away to a band called the Third Republic.

100 YEARS AGO

THE GOLD

RUSH

At the end of the nineteenth century large numbers of excited Americans were frequently to be seen rushing headlong towards holes in the ground, hoping to find gold. Most of them never even found the holes in the ground. But at least they all had a good day, with plenty of exercise and fresh air, which kept them healthy. And health is much more valuable than gold ... well, nearly more valuable ... isn't it?

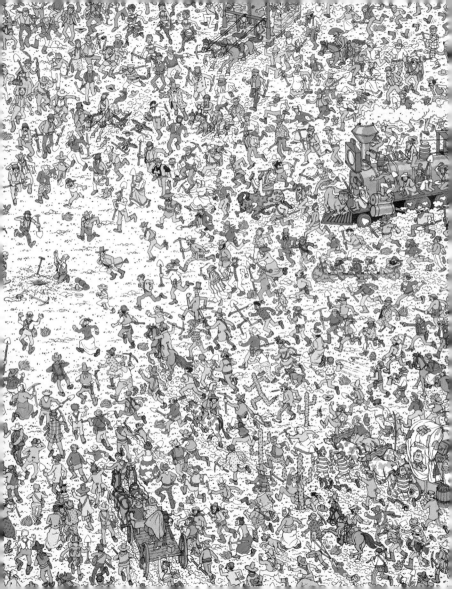

THE GREAT WHERE'S WALLY NOW? CHECK LIST
Hundreds more things for time travellers to look for!

THE STONE AGE
- Four cavemen swinging into trouble
- An accident with an axe
- A great invention
- A Stone-Age rodeo
- Boars chasing a man
- Men chasing a boar
- A romantic caveman
- A mammoth squirt
- A man who has overeaten
- A bear trap
- A mammoth in the river
- A fruit stall
- Charging woolly rhinos
- A big cover-up
- A trunk holding a trunk
- A knockout game of baseball
- A rocky picture show
- An upside-down boar
- A spoilt dog
- A lesson on dinosaurs
- A very scruffy family
- Some dangerous spear fishermen

THE RIDDLE OF THE PYRAMIDS
- An upside-down pyramid
- An upside-down sarcophagus
- A group of posing gods
- Two protruding hands
- Two protruding feet
- A fat man and his picture
- Seventeen protruding tongues
- Stones defying gravity
- Egyptian vandals
- Egyptian graffiti
- A man sweeping dirt under a pyramid
- A thirsty sphinx
- A runaway block of stone
- Two weedy builders
- A cheeky builder
- A picture firing an arrow
- A careless water-carrier
- Sunbathers in peril
- A messy milking session
- A mummy and a baby
- Pyramids of sand

FUN AND GAMES IN ANCIENT ROME
- A charioteer who has lost his chariot
- Coliseum cleaners
- An unequal contest with spears
- A winner who is about to lose
- A lion with good table manners
- A deadly set of wheels
- Lion cubs being teased
- Four shields that match their owners
- A pyramid of lions
- Lions giving the paws down
- A leopard chasing a leopard skin
- A piggyback puncher
- An awful musician
- A painful fork-lift
- A horse holding the reins
- A leopard in love
- A Roman keeping count
- A gladiator losing his sandals

ON TOUR WITH THE VIKINGS
- A happy figurehead
- Figureheads in love
- A man being used as a club
- A tearful sheep
- Two hopeless hiding places
- Childish Vikings
- A beard with a foot on it
- An eagle posing as a helmet
- A sailor tearing a sail
- A heavily armed Viking
- A patchy couple
- Three spears being beheaded
- A burning behind
- A bent boat
- A frightened figurehead
- Locked horns
- A helmet with spiders
- A helmet of smoke
- A bullfight

THE END OF THE CRUSADES
- A cat about to be catapulted
- A man about to be catapulted
- A human bridge
- A key that's out of reach
- A message for the milkman
- A cauldron of boiling oil
- A battering-ram
- Crusaders caught by their necks
- A load of washing
- Two catapult catastrophes
- A catapult aiming the wrong way
- Three snakes
- A crusader fast asleep
- Crusaders soaking up the sun
- Flattened crusaders
- Rockfaces
- A crusader who broke a ladder
- A ticklish situation

ONCE UPON A SATURDAY MORNING
- A dirty downpour
- Archers missing the target
- A jouster sitting back to front
- A dog stalking a cat stalking some birds
- A long line of pickpockets
- A jouster who needs lots of practice
- A man making a bear dance
- A bear making a man dance
- Hats that are tied together
- Fruit and vegetable thieves
- An unexpected puddle
- A juggling jester
- A very long drink
- A heavily burdened beast
- Drunken friars
- A man scything hats
- An angry fish
- A ticklish torture
- Minstrels making an awful noise